The Big

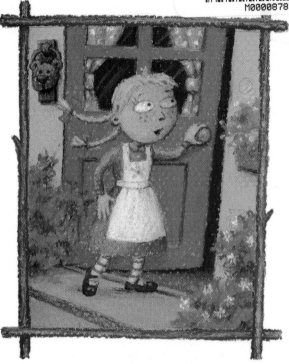

by Lada Kratky
illustrated by Lynne Chapman

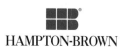

HAMPTON-BROWN

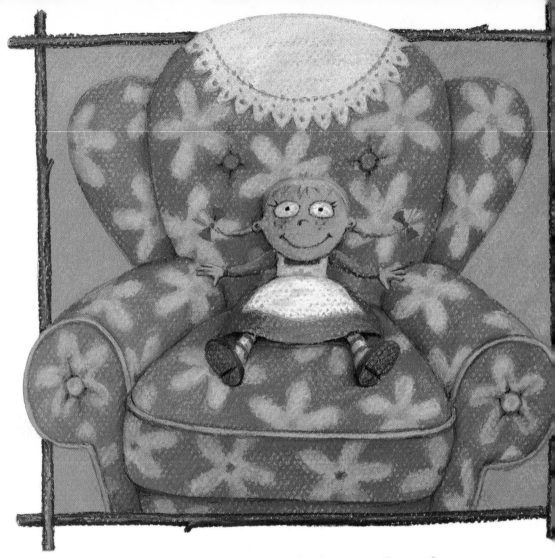

This is a big chair.

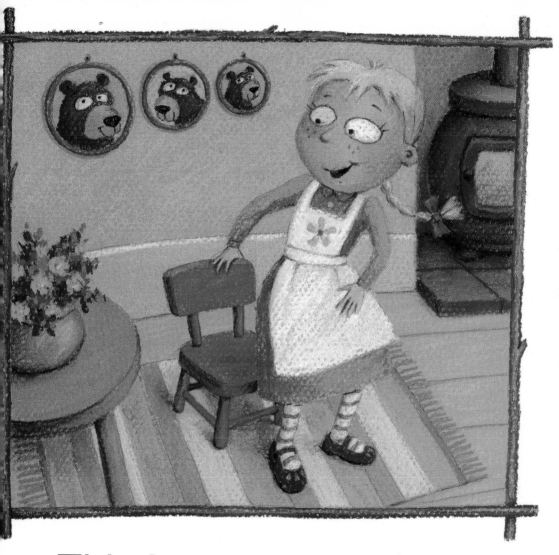

This is not a big chair.

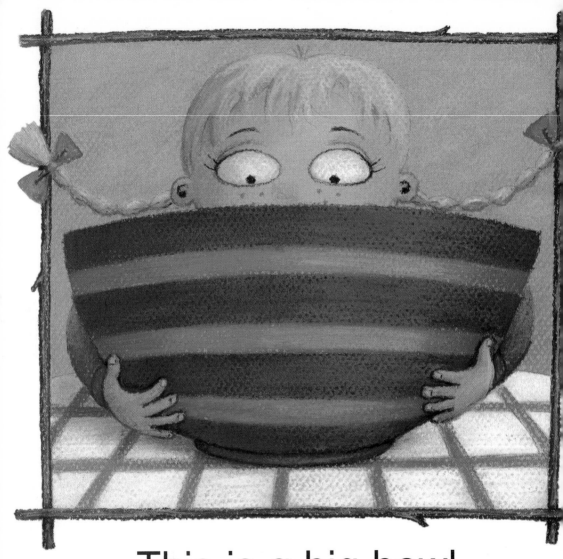

This is a big bowl.

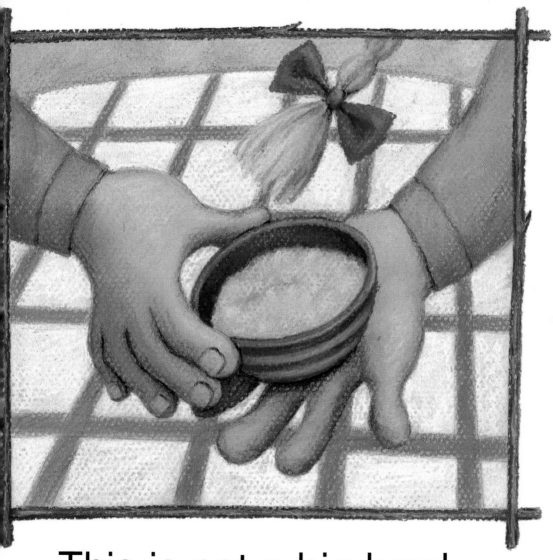

This is not a big bowl.

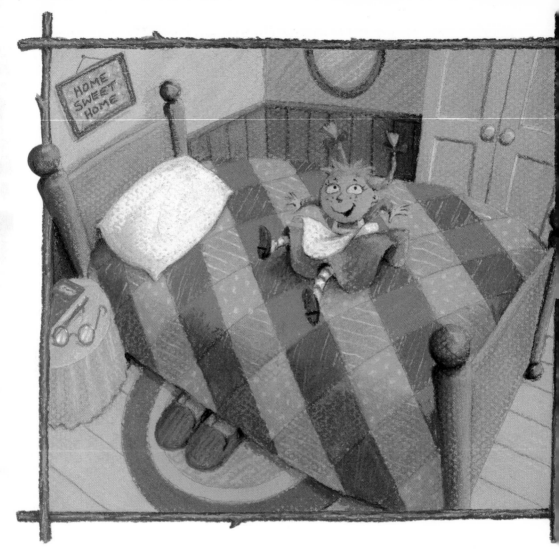

This is a big bed.

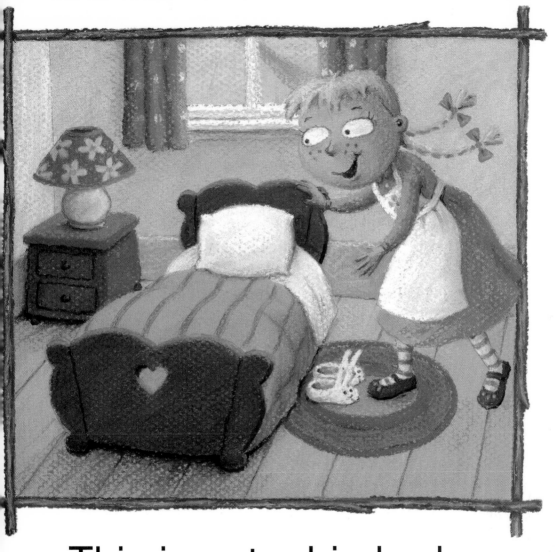

This is not a big bed.

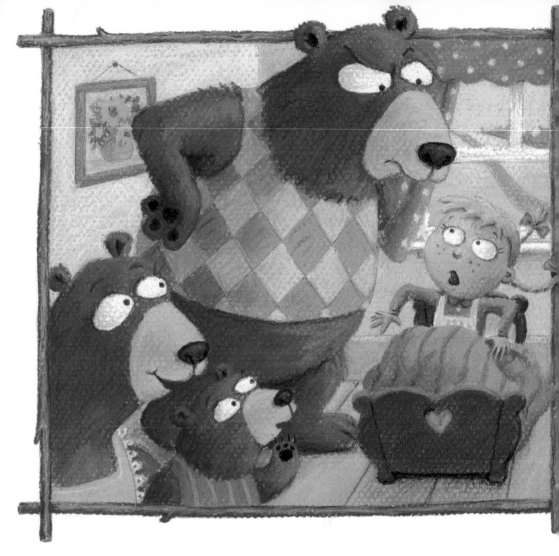

Oh no! This is a BIG bear!

8